"This generation of Christia[...] only biblical revelation about reality but also the reality of reality itself. The Questions for Restless Minds series poses many of the toughest questions faced by young Christians to some of the world's foremost Christian thinkers and leaders. Along the way, this series seeks to help the Christian next generation to learn how to think biblically when they face questions in years to come that perhaps no one yet sees coming."

—**Russell Moore,**
public theologian, *Christianity Today*

"If you're hungry to go deeper in your faith, wrestle with hard questions, and are dissatisfied with the shallow content on your social media newsfeed, you'll really appreciate this series of thoughtful deep dives on critically important topics like faith, the Bible, friendship, sexuality, philosophy, and more. As you engage with some world-class Christian scholars, you'll be encouraged, equipped, challenged, and above all invited to love God more with your heart, soul, mind, and strength."

—**Andy Kim,**
multiethnic resource director, InterVarsity Christian Fellowship

How Do We Live
in a Digital World?

Questions for Restless Minds

Questions for Restless Minds

QUESTIONS FOR RESTLESS MINDS

How Do We Live in a Digital World?

C. Ben Mitchell

D. A. Carson,
Series Editor

LEXHAM PRESS

How Do We Live in a Digital World?
Questions for Restless Minds, edited by D. A. Carson

Copyright 2021 Christ on Campus Initiative

Lexham Press, 1313 Commercial St., Bellingham, WA 98225
LexhamPress.com

Print ISBN 9781683595311
Digital ISBN 9781683595328
Library of Congress Control Number 2021937698

Lexham Editorial: Todd Hains, Abigail Stocker, Mandi Newell
Cover Design: Brittany Schrock
Interior Design and Typesetting: Abigail Stocker, ProjectLuz.com

The Christ on Campus Initiative exists to inspire students on college and university campuses to think wisely, act with conviction, and become more Christlike by providing relevant and excellent evangelical resources on contemporary issues.

Visit christoncampuscci.org.

TRINITY
EVANGELICAL DIVINITY SCHOOL
TRINITY INTERNATIONAL UNIVERSITY

Contents

Series Preface

D. A. CARSON, SERIES EDITOR

T HE ORIGIN OF this series of books lies with a group of faculty from Trinity Evangelical Divinity School (TEDS), under the leadership of Scott Manetsch. We wanted to address topics faced by today's undergraduates, especially those from Christian homes and churches.

If you are one such student, you already know what we have in mind. You know that most churches, however encouraging they may be, are not equipped to prepare you for what you will face when you enroll at university.

It's not as if you've never known any winsome atheists before going to college; it's not as if you've never thought about Islam, or the credibility of the New Testament documents, or the nature of friendship, or gender identity, or how the claims of Jesus sound too exclusive and rather narrow, or the nature of evil. But up until now you've probably thought about such things within the shielding cocoon of a community of faith.

Now you are at college, and the communities in which you are embedded often find Christian perspectives to be at best oddly quaint and old-fashioned, if not repulsive. To use the current jargon, it's easy to become socialized into a new community, a new world.

How shall you respond? You could, of course, withdraw a little: just buckle down and study computer science or Roman history (or whatever your subject is) and refuse to engage with others. Or you could throw over your Christian heritage as something that belongs to your immature years and buy into the cultural package that surrounds you. Or—and this is what we hope you will do—you could become better informed.

But how shall you go about this? On any disputed topic, you do not have the time, and probably not the interest, to bury yourself in a couple of dozen volumes written by experts for experts. And if you did, that would be on *one* topic—and there are scores of topics that will grab the attention of the inquisitive student. On the other hand, brief pamphlets with predictable answers couched in safe slogans will prove to be neither attractive nor convincing.

So we have adopted a middle course. We have written short books pitched at undergraduates who want arguments that are accessible and stimulating, but invariably courteous. The material is comprehensive enough that it has become an important resource for pastors and other campus leaders who devote their energies to work with students. Each book ends with a brief annotated bibliography and study questions, intended for readers who want to probe a little further.

Lexham Press is making this series available both as attractive books and digitally in new formats (ebook and Logos resource). We hope and pray you will find them helpful and convincing.

INTRODUCTION

W E WERE HAVING an early dinner at one of our favorite mom-and-pop restaurants in a sleepy little Southern town just outside where we live. As Nancy and I were talking about our day, a lad about twelve years old came through the door with an older woman who appeared to be his grandmother. It was as close to a Norman Rockwell scene as one might imagine. Grandmother and grandson were out for a quiet meal together on a Friday evening. One could even imagine this being a weekly treat for them both, a regular liturgy of life in this tiny community.

The owner of the restaurant is also the cook. His wife waits tables, delivering daily specials, superb hamburgers, or house-made pizzas to mostly local customers who sit at Formica-top tables while drinking sweet tea and watching the sparse traffic pass by on the other side of the plateglass windows of the storefront restaurant. The scene was about as bucolic as it gets these days. It could just as easily have been 1956 as 2016. Except.

As we waited for our burger baskets, I noticed that the young lad was using a smartphone. That's not unusual for someone his age or, for that matter, any age these days. His grandmother quickly surveyed the menu, asked the boy what he wanted to eat, and placed the order. The lad never looked up from his phone. I mean he *never* looked up from his phone. While he and his grandmother waited for their order, both of his thumbs were busy on the phone. Meanwhile, the grandmother gazed from one direction to another, trying to find something to interest her while the lad played on. He never looked up. When their meals arrived, he switched from two hands on the phone to one hand on the phone and one hand holding his hamburger. He did not look up for the entire twenty minutes it took him to bolt down that sandwich. After they had both eaten their meals, the boy followed his grandmother out of the restaurant, still never looking up from his phone.

What could have been an emotionally bonding experience between a grandmother and her grandson, turned out to be dinner alone, together. Instead of receiving the wisdom of her years of life experience, the lad spent all his time on a digital device. The most disheartening reality of this picture is that we've all seen or experienced something similar and it's not as disturbing to us as it ought to be. Familiarity has eroded contempt. Or, at the very least, we have no idea what to do about it, so we just move on while the proverbial water boils the frog in the kettle.

Digital technology is here to stay. And on our best days, I don't think we'd want it to go away. We've become quite comfortable with digital technologies and even dependent on many of them. We like the speed, efficiency, and connectivity they offer. We have come to depend on a quick text message, an informative email, or an entertaining meme on Facebook. As the number of so-called digital natives continues to swell—those individuals born after 1980 who have always had access to computers, laptops, tablets, smartphones, and whatever is next—rapid adoption of new digital technologies will continue to be the norm rather than the exception.

Yet despite the number of technologies we use, there seems to be large-scale naivete about technology's effects, especially the impact of digital technologies. Even otherwise helpful theologians and social analysts sometimes make the unsophisticated claim that technologies are morally neutral; that in and of themselves they are neither good nor bad, but it is the use of the technology that may be right or wrong. If it were that simple, answers to our questions would be much simpler. Unfortunately, the morality of technology is more complicated than we have imagined. Emerging biotechnologies—like genetic augmentation, artificial intelligence, cybernetics, and robotics, for instance—mean that the human technologist may become the technology, the engineer may become the engineered. That is, beings themselves may become the artifacts of biotechnological innovation. More about that later.

As Stephen Monsma and his colleagues at Calvin College pointed out decades ago in their book *Responsible Technology*,[1] and the French philosopher Jacques Ellul[2] before them, technologies are hardly value neutral. That is not to presume that technology is by nature evil. Far from it. But every tool has an impact on its user and the choice to develop and adopt any technology is a morally freighted choice. We must assume

5

that the technology makes life better or we would most likely reject it. And since "better" implies some notion of the good life, the invention and adoption of a particular technology is informed by certain values, almost always nowadays the notion that efficiency is better than inefficiency and that faster is necessarily better than slower.

Despite the fact that we make certain choices about technology, as founding editor of WIRED magazine, Kevin Kelly, has put it, there seems to be an inevitability about it. Some people even speak of a kind of technological determinism; if the technology exists we must use it. Although technological determinism may overstate the case, Kelly's point is that there is a certain momentum to technological developments, including digital innovation, that continues to propel them. "The strong tides that shaped digital technologies for the past 30 years," he predicts, "will continue to expand and harden in the next 30 years."[3] If he's right, and I suspect he is, where is technology going, and what will our technoculture look like in thirty years? These are profound questions, especially for Christians who, as the apostle Paul said, are not to be conformed to the world, but to be transformed by the renewing of our minds (Rom 12:2).

Let's begin with where we are today. The accumulated data are breathtaking. According to the World Economic Forum's report, *Digital Media and Society: Implications in a Hyperconnected Era*,[4] in 2015 there were approximately 3 billion internet users, 2 billion active social media users, and more than 1.6 billion mobile social accounts.

Consumers of digital media spend increasing amounts of time with their digital devices:

- People now spend an average of 2 hours daily on the mobile web.

- Individuals devote 1.8 hours to social networking, 30 percent of their daily online time.

- Digital natives spend on average more than 7 hours per day on their smartphones or on multiple digital devices (often at the same time).

- The average "frequent user" is young, male, well educated, and father of one child.

- By the second quarter of 2016, Facebook had 1.71 billion active users.

- WhatsApp users grew from 700 million worldwide in 2015 to 1 billion by February 2016.

- WeChat dominates social media in China, with over 697 million users.

- The average user is bombarded by more than 1,700 banner ads per month.

These are stunning numbers that give some people vertigo and others a mild adrenaline rush. What might all of this mean for the future? Where are we going? Are we being led by market forces and insatiable human desire, or are we making carefully informed choices about digital media? And how are Christians to think about these things?

First, I want to outline some of the opportunities that digital media offer individuals, society, Christians, and their churches. Then, in the context of what we know about our anthropology—what it means to be human—I want to say something about the challenges these new technologies bring. Then, I will offer some recommendations based on the findings.

For the record, I am neither a technological optimist nor a technological pessimist. I am a critical realist who thinks we should make informed judgments. Furthermore, I am a personalist[5] who believes that persons take priority over things. In that same spirit of full disclosure, I should reveal that I am not a digital native but a digital immigrant. That is, I grew up before the advent of contemporary digital technology. For some, this fact may disqualify me from the conversation. Rather than disqualify me, however, in her excellent volume *i-Minds,* clinical neuropsychologist Mari Swingle points out that "one advantage digital immigrants do have is that of perspective: we all have been witnesses to great changes in ourselves and the generation(s) that came after us."[6] So, for whatever it may be worth, I will offer my perspective as a digital immigrant.

Although I had owned a personal computer for several years prior, I vividly remember less than forty years ago connecting for the first time to my university's UNIVAC system through a telephone dial-up connection. Those were the days of the CRT (cathode-ray tube) screen with a black background and amber letters. Users had to boot up their computer, enter a telephone number, and listen to a screeching noise that sounded a lot like some kind of sadistic cat torture as a desktop computer with two three-and-a-half-inch disk drives was connected by telephone line to a mainframe computer housed in a specially air-conditioned room somewhere in the belly of the campus. If someone else had already connected through that telephone number, you got a busy signal and had to try another number. If that number was also busy, you had to wait until the line was free again.

I was just beginning doctoral work in 1989. Although connection to the internet was less than instantaneous, the ability to send and receive email, participate in list serves, and communicate through synchronous chat were thrilling developments. I remember my amazement the first time I had an onscreen live-chat with another graduate student. I was in Tennessee and she was in Israel. I would type a line or two, wait 10–20 seconds, and see her lines appear on my screen 10–20 seconds after she typed them. As primitive and app-less as it all seems now, science fiction became science fact right before my very eyes.

But I noticed that something else happened along the way. I remember reading, reflecting, and writing for many uninterrupted hours at a time during graduate school days. Because everyone else was working hard too, there were

9

few distractions in the graduate student apartment complex. When I did take the time to endure the relatively elaborate and time-consuming procedure to check email or visit the list serve, there would only be a few new entries in any twenty-four-hour period. I would check email once or twice a day, not only because it took so long to get connected, but because the rewards would be slim. Connectivity was less than instantaneous, and information was less than abundant.

Since confession is good for the soul, I will tell you, frankly, that my attention span is not what it was before digital technology. The siren call of email, Facebook, Twitter, Pinterest, and a hundred other apps now beckons us every hour of the day and night. I receive more email in an hour than I did for entire days during graduate school. My email program notifies me of the delivery of each new communication with an audible alert. Many people who don't want to wait on a returned email now text me expecting a more immediate response.

There is exponentially more content on the internet today than in 1991, when the first webpage appeared. In terms of volume, the internet quadrupled in size between 2014 and the end of 2016. More than 1.3 zettabytes of data are transported between computer networks worldwide— that's 1.3 followed with 20 zeros. By 2020 that number was estimated to grow to 40 zettabytes. That number is so large it's difficult to comprehend.

Among other things, all of this means that it is increasingly challenging in our digital age to concentrate for multiple minutes, much less hours at a time without interruption, admittedly, often self-imposed interruption. Although I will grant that my experience cannot be taken to be universal, I suspect that there are plenty of others who can empathize. What does all of this mean for the future of digital communication? What does all of this mean for Christians and for the church?

2

THE OPPORTUNITIES OF DIGITAL TECHNOLOGIES

WE SHOULD NOTE, *firstly, that the internet has done much to connect people, give them a voice, and facilitate the creation of virtual communities that have the opportunity to shape real communities.* Many will remember the role digital media played in the ouster of Tunisian president Zine El Abidine Ben Ali and the overthrow of Hosni Mubarak in the so-called Arab Spring of 2011. Social media had an important part in building activist networks and rallying protesters, especially in Egypt. If literacy is power, connectivity is shared power.

Similarly, digital media have united religious believers and religious communities around the world. In her work on media and religion, Texas A&M professor of communication, Heidi Campbell, chronicles the evolution of what she and her colleagues have coined "digital religion."[7] Although Christian and Muslim adherents are thought to occupy the greatest bandwidth in social media, Hindu, Buddhist, and new Japanese religions have a growing footprint in the digital landscape. Through phenomena like the birth of religious user groups, broadcast-style web forums, and the founding of cyberchurches and virtual interactive worship environments, the internet has provided a new media context for religious expression, proselytism, and engagement. And, as Campbell and others have pointed out, it is a two-way street. That is, not only are new media being shaped by religious communities, but religious communities are being shaped by new media. Notions of authority, authenticity, community, identity, ritual, and religion are all being shaped and re-shaped, formed and informed by digital religion.

In his introduction to *Ministry in the Digital Age*, Biola University's David Bourgeois maintains that "the Internet is the greatest communication tool ever invented by humans,"[8] and that "the single most important thing you can do for your ministry's use of the Internet and social media is to design, document and implement a digital strategy."[9] For him, one of the most strategic activities in which a church can engage is the creation of a "digital ministry framework ... that will allow you to be confident that your use of digital technologies is on the right track."[10]

According to a 2010 random survey of Protestant churches by Axletree Media in conjunction with the research arm of Lifeway, 78 percent of churches maintain a website. Of those websites, 91 percent provided information to potential visitors to the church, 79 percent provided information for the congregation, 57 percent encouraged increased participation by members of the church, and 52 percent solicited interest in ministries or volunteer opportunities.[11] A 2015 Barna Group study, *Cyber Church: Pastors and the Internet*, found that 96 percent of pastors use a computer at church, 46 percent use it for email, and 39 percent use it to access the internet.[12] Among those pastors who use the internet at church, 97 percent use it to find information, 88 percent to buy products, 80 percent to keep up with existing relationships, 71 percent to check out new music or videos, 39 percent to have a spiritual or religious experience, and 11 percent to play video games.

In 2015 the Church of England announced that they would equip all of its sixteen thousand churches with Wi-Fi internet access. The idea was first suggested by composer Andrew Lloyd Webber, who said that "connecting churches to the internet would make them the centres of their communities once again to draw more visitors to these sites and encourage churches to enhance and develop outreach programs to serve the practical and spiritual needs of a digital generation."[13] The point is that, for good or ill, digital media are increasingly integrated into the life of the churches and their ministers.

In her newest volume, *Networked Theology: Negotiating Faith in Digital Culture,* Campbell and her coauthor, New Zealand theologian Stephen Garner, argue it is crucial that we ask, "What is it ... that the Christian tradition can offer here in light of the good news of Jesus Christ? And how can it offer it in a way that is intelligible and credible to those in that context and also valuable and relevant to their everyday lives? All of these factors are critical for our theologizing about technology and media if it is to have a very real presence."[14]

Secondly, digital media are also changing the way we obtain information. Through the internet we now live in what amounts to a single, worldwide virtual library. Receptive knowledge, or what University of Connecticut philosopher Michael Patrick Lynch calls "Google-knowing,"[15] is available to anyone who can use a computer or other digital device that can connect to the internet. Information retrieval is much easier than it used to be.

As an experiment, Lynch says that he wrote down four rather random questions to which he wanted answers:

1. What is the capital of Bulgaria?

2. Is a four-stroke outboard engine more efficient than a two-stroke?

3. What is the phone number of my US representative?

4. What is the best-reviewed restaurant in Austin, Texas, this week?

He tried to answer those questions without resorting to digital sources. He pulled a dictionary from his shelves, located a map, and confirmed that Sofia was the capital of Bulgaria. He worried, however, that the information might be inaccurate given the publication date of his dictionary and the fluidity of eastern Europe.

Question 2 was more difficult, not least because he didn't have any boat engine manuals. So he went to a local marina and consulted a mechanic. He got his answer after some effort and depending on whether or not the mechanic actually knew what he was talking about.

Though he thought Question 3 would be easiest, he remembered that he no longer owned a phone book. And when he went to his local library, instead of pointing him to a telephone book, the person behind the counter suggested that he use the computer to find out. After finally locating a telephone book on the library shelves, he discovered his answer, despite the fact that it could have been wrong since it was several years old.

Question 4 proved to be the most difficult because he did not know anyone in Austin, Texas. He thought about calling the local chamber of commerce, but he didn't have any way to get their number. Besides, there was no reason to think the chamber would necessarily know the answer to such a timely question. Since his local library in Connecticut did not have any Texas newspapers, he was stymied. The best restaurant in Austin that week remained elusive.

I just replicated his experiment using the internet and found the answers to all the questions in about two minutes. "Speed is the most obvious distinguishing character-istic of how we know now," says Lynch. "Google-knowing is fast."[16] Lynch points out that because of the speed and contemporaneous nature of the data, we increasingly trust digitally acquired information over other sources of infor-mation—whether or not that trust is truly warranted. More about that later.

Books, encyclopedias, dictionaries, news, and commentaries are available with a simple mouse click or touch of a fingertip on a digital app on a mobile device. Although sales of e-readers dropped to 12 million in 2015 from 20 million in 2011, most books today are published in both digital and print formats. According to a 2015 Nielsen survey, 32 percent of people read books primarily on e-readers. Even libraries are finding digital holdings to be popular among patrons. The library in Brevard County, Florida, lent 1 million digital materials (ebooks, e-audiobooks, and periodicals) between August 2011 and October 2016.

Thirdly, digital media are changing the way work gets done in business. A Pew Research Center study published in 2014, pointed out that 94 percent of the US job force are internet users. Sixty-one percent of adult internet users said that email was "very important" to doing their job, while 54 percent said the internet itself was very important for their jobs. Somewhat surprisingly, just 7 percent of working online adults feel their productivity has dropped because of the internet, email and cell phones, while 46 percent feel more productive. Fifty-one percent of those surveyed said that the internet expanded the number of people with whom they communicate outside of their company, and 39 percent said that the internet allowed more flexibility in the hours they worked, while 35 percent said the internet increased the number of hours they worked. [17]

According to a 2016 report from Deloitte, the multinational professional services firm, "Today's growth in technological capabilities, exponential increase in computing power available to both consumers and enterprises, and almost ubiquitous Internet connectivity among other digital advances is changing the way employees and enterprises work." Faster computing speed and greater storage is making virtual and global collaboration possible in more fields every day. As digital technology becomes more robust and hardware more reliable, employers become more comfortable with employees working on their devices instead of meeting face-to-face or coming into an office. Deloitte suggests that since millennials are the first truly "digital native" generation, they should get special attention when it comes to technology in the workplace. After all, the U.S. Bureau of Labor Statistics predicts that by 2030 millennials will make up 75 percent of the workforce. "As millennials grow into managerial roles, their priorities—i.e., working for more than just a paycheck—and leadership styles will have a huge impact on all organizations in the coming years."[18] Obviously, then, new media are playing pivotal roles in the economy. In fact, the nearly universal penetration of digital media in business has been tagged by some business leaders and social commentators "the third industrial revolution."

In many of the same ways, digital media are changing the way churches, synagogues, mosques, and temples do their business. Shane Hipps, the lead pastor of Trinity Mennonite Church in Phoenix, offers an *apologia* for the use of digital technology in his book *Flickering Pixels:*

How Technology Shapes Your Faith. The book, says Hipps, "explores the hidden power of media and technology as a way to understand who we are, who we think God is, and how God's unchanging message has changed, is changing, and will change"[19] as a result of the mosaic of flickering pixels. Borrowing Marshall McLuhan's famous aphorism, "the medium is the message," Hipps argues that "Jesus *is* God's perfect medium—and the medium *is* the message."[20] Since Jesus embodies God's grace and mercy, and since the church is the body of Christ, by extension Christians "are the message," a message of healing and hope to the world.[21] Social media becomes a strategic way for the church to bear witness to God's grace and to serve others in his name.

From a sociological and communications standpoint, technology and religious groups are so thoroughly integrated that "digital religion" is now something to be studied. Religious expression on the internet has moved far beyond digitized sermons, Christian chat rooms, and livestreamed worship services. Campbell explains,

> With the rise of the virtual world many groups are embracing technologies such as Second Life to create an online worship experience that offers an interactive worship via avatars (for example the Anglican Cathedral in Second Life, or the Church of Fools). Now we see the Internet becoming a tool to extend a church's offline ministry into online spaces. For instance, we see the rise of Internet campuses

within many multisite churches, and webcasting of services via iPhone and Facebook apps (for example LifeChurch.tv) becoming common. Thus, rather than being an alternative social space for a few, digital technology becomes an important platform extending and altering religious practice for many.[22]

Digital media can facilitate education and lifelong learning. Online education is a growth industry thanks to the internet. According to a 2016 report by *Forbes*, "more than 35 million people have enrolled in online courses in the last four years, and 2015 enrollments doubled from 2014. (That's equal to one out of five working professionals in the U.S.!)" Today there are more than 4,200 MOOC courses available (many more if you include the corporate training programs from companies like Udemy, BigThink, Pluralsight, Lynda, NovoEd, and Skillsoft)."[23] For more about the interesting ways that digital media are changing the world of education, see the article, "How 'Elite' Universities Are Using Online Education."[24]

3

THE
CHALLENGES OF
DIGITAL MEDIA

INFORMATION RETRIEVAL, ECONOMIC growth, digital religion, and access to education represent significant sectors of opportunity that the burgeoning digital revolution is helping us realize. As with nearly every other arena of life, however, there are both benefits and burdens. An accurate benefits versus burdens calculus may help us determine whether or not digital media are a net gain or a net loss; but it may well turn out to be more complex than that. Perhaps the gains are sufficiently robust to justify ongoing technological development, but instead of uncritical adoption, we should develop criteria for making better informed choices. How would we begin to do that? What should we know that will help us make good choices about technology?

Let's begin with this question: Does digital technology contribute to human flourishing? Surely this is an important question for any technology, and not least one that is so clearly poised, according to some futurists, to tempt us to jettison our humanity. Here, of course, I'm thinking not only about transhumanists,[25] but also any who are tempted to believe in a kind of technological inevitability that will eventually outgrow human capacities and require us either to fight for our very lives or succumb to servitude to the Machine. Just so, sociologist Katherine Hayles has written, "Humans can either go quietly into that good night, joining the dinosaurs as a species that once ruled the earth but is now obsolete, or hang on for a little while longer by becoming machines themselves. In either case ... the age of the human is drawing to a close."[26]

What sorts of creatures are we humans? And what does human flourishing look like in a burgeoning digital "technoculture"? What burdens do digital technologies pose for human well-being? These are profound questions in this phase of the twenty-first century.

We are innovators. The proliferation of digital media, like other technological innovation, demonstrates that *Homo sapiens* (human knowers) are also by nature *Homo faber* (human makers). What economist Michael Novak has called "the fire of invention"[27] burns in the belly of human beings. In the beginning, "The LORD God took the man and put him in the Garden of Eden to work it and keep it" (Gen 2:15). God's mandate to Adam and all his progeny to "have dominion over the fish of the sea and over the birds of the heavens and over every living thing that moves on the earth," extended to every non-living thing too (Gen 1:28). Indeed, in the Genesis story we find people making tools, boats, weapons, and cities. Sometimes called "the cultural mandate," this injunction is a tacit directive to create technologies and culture.

Creativity is one of those attributes that God shares with his human creatures. And create we must. Inventiveness and innovation are woven into the very fabric of our natures. So we develop, improve, conquer, subdue, and steward natural and other resources, including our own bodies. Generally speaking, we should celebrate, cultivate, and reward creativity as a divine gift.

We are social. From the beginning human beings both desired and found benefits in community. Although God saw that everything else was good in his new creation, it was not good that man should be alone (Gen 2). Technology has contributed in unparalleled ways to help humans build community. From the family farm to the construction of small towns and large cities, we demonstrate that we are social creatures. Sewage treatment, electricity, telephones, computers, and technologies like WiFi, help us manage population-dense communities. Connectivity is a buzz word today because, among other things, it emphasizes our commitment to cultivating social networks of people across extremely diverse locations, populations, and cultures.

We are playful. Play is a natural expression of our creativity and sociability. Put two human beings together and give them a moment's release from the burden to survive, and they will develop games and competitions. Doubtless Adam and Eve played hide and seek in the garden. Josef Pieper has argued convincingly that leisure is the basis of culture. At its best, entertainment is a form of leisure—rest for the soul against the pressures of worry, the hurry-up culture, and the burdens of duty. Technology not only helps us find more time for leisure by doing some chores more efficiently, but digital technologies have also become an enormous source of entertainment. Radio, television, video games, and web-based social networks are ubiquitous forms of entertainment in most parts of the world.

We make choices. Humans are willing beings. Philosopher of technology, David Nye, reminds us that, "Machines are not like meteors that come unbidden from outside and have an 'impact.' Rather, human beings make choices when inventing, marketing, and using a new device."[28] Although it sometimes feels like there is a kind of inevitability about technology, we can and do resist certain technologies. Just because we *can* do something doesn't mean that we *should*, much less that we *must*. Even when a ubiquitous digital technology like text messaging is so pervasive, that does not mean we are determined to check our phones every second. But, as sociologist Sherry Turkle says, this takes the will to "both redesign technology and change how we bring it into our lives."

We are desiring beings. Our desires, our loves, our affections are expressed in our habits. To borrow one of the titles of Jamie Smith's books, *You Are What You Love*.[29] Or as St. Augustine taught, sin is disordered desire, disordered love. The Christian life is one of re-ordering our desires to bring them in conformity with the love of God. We should love God with our whole hearts, love our neighbors as ourselves, and enjoy God through our relationship with him and through the things he has made. Jesus said, "The good person out of the good treasure of his heart produces good, and the evil person out of his evil treasure produces evil, for out of the abundance of the heart his mouth speaks" (Luke 6:45).

We are embodied. All humans are embodied beings. From conception to death, and from resurrection throughout eternity, to be human means to have a body. We learn this not only from the Genesis account where we are told that God made Adam's body from the dust of the earth (Gen 2:7), we learn it supremely in the coming of the God-man, Jesus Christ. "Offspring of a Virgin's womb," as we sing during the Christmas season, Jesus is perfect God and perfect man. From his conception, Jesus is an embodied human person. Or, as the apostle John put it in his account of the good news of Jesus, "the Word became flesh and dwelt among us, and we have seen his glory, glory as of the only Son from the Father, full of grace and truth" (John 1:14). Through the incarnation—the enfleshment of God in Jesus Christ—God sacralizes the human body. Our humanity is a bodily state of existence just as Jesus' humanity is a bodily state of existence. Radical dualism is not only mistaken anthropology, it is mistaken Christology.

We are limited and fallen. In short, we are not God. In fact, our Lenten confession is that from dust we have come, and to dust we shall return. Despite the many marvelous human accomplishments, we are limited, mortal creatures. God alone is omnipresent, omnipotent, and omniscient. We are limited by time and space—we can only be genuinely present in one place at a time. We are limited in our powers—mental, emotional, spiritual, and physical. We are limited in our knowledge—including our native intelligence and memory, so we are unable to anticipate every possible consequence of our decisions. Moreover, we are not only morally limited so that we do not always choose what is best for us, but also because of our sinfulness, we sometimes choose that which is ultimately harmful to ourselves and others. So we petition God to forgive both our sins of commission and our sins of omission.

A NEW TOWER OF BABEL

The dual plagues of naivete on the one hand and hubris on the other have often resulted in profound harm to individuals, communities, and societies. The Tower of Babel looms large as an example of human pride (Gen 11:1–9). In his most helpful volume, *Virtual Morality: Christian Ethics in the Computer Age*, Graham Houston observes:

> The ziggurat is a well-known feature of ancient Mesopotamia, and was often built with mud bricks and tar due to the scarcity of local stone. It is therefore a symbol of technology-gone-wrong, the result of the ingenuity of humankind in culling materials and using them for their own evil purposes. But it is also a symbol of their pride, their desire to make a name for themselves (11:4). Excavated inscriptions indicate that these towers were meant to serve as stairways to heaven. They had a purely religious significance and had no practical use apart from religious ritual. According to the biblical narrative, they were symbolic of the desire to usurp the authority

of the landlord. They were declarations of independence from the true God, yet also expressions of underlying religious needs.

Since the fall in the garden, the proclivities of humanity are toward rebellion against God, often manifest as the desire to be gods ourselves. Although they are expressive of our creativity, technologies have also provided the means for us to feel more self-sufficient and less dependent on God. In many ways we have become masters of our own fate, developing life-saving technologies like chemotherapy, coronary artery bypass grafts, and organ transplants. We can now stave off the ravages of disease. The tower grows taller. Next is immortality and human perfection, or is it?

Yuval Noah Harari is professor of history at the Hebrew University of Jerusalem and author of the award-winning volume *Sapiens: A Brief History of Humankind*. In his sequel, *Homo Deus: A Brief History of Tomorrow*, he declares:

> In the early 21st century the train of progress is again pulling out of the station—and this will probably be the last train ever to leave the station called *Homo sapiens*. Those who miss this train will never get a second chance. In order to get a seat on it, you need to understand 21st century technology, and in particular the powers of biotechnology and computer algorithms.
>
> … These powers are far more potent than steam and the telegraph, and they will not be used mainly

for the production of food, textiles, vehicles and weapons. The main products of the 21st century will be bodies, brains and minds, and the gap between those who know how to engineer bodies and brains and those who do not will be wider than the gap between Dickens's Britain and the Madhi's Sudan. Indeed, it will be bigger than the gap between *Sapiens* and Neanderthals. In the 21st century, those who ride the train of progress will acquire divine abilities of creation and destruction, while those left behind will face extinction.[30]

Harari maintains that humanity's new religion is what he calls "dataism," the worldview that all of reality can be reduced to numbers. Those data are immense and are growing at a rate humans simply cannot keep up with. "Dataists are skeptical about human knowledge and wisdom," he suggests, "and prefer to put their trust in Big Data and computer algorithms."[31] He ends up predicting a dystopian future, in part because resistance is futile. "You may not agree with the idea that organisms are algorithms, and that giraffes, tomatoes and human beings are just different methods of processing data. But you should know that this is the current scientific dogma, and that it is changing our world beyond recognition."[32]

Changes in our humanity will not happen overnight:

34

Homo sapiens is likely to upgrade itself step by step, merging with robots and computers in the process, until our descendants look back and realise that they are no longer the kind of animal that wrote the Bible, built the Great Wall of China and laughed at Charlie Chaplin's antics. This will not happen in a day, or a year. Indeed, it is already happening right now, through innumerable mundane actions. Every day millions of people decide to grant their smartphone a bit more control over their lives or try a new and more effective antidepressant drug. In pursuit of health, happiness, and power, humans will gradually change first one of their features and then another, and another, until they will no longer be human.[33]

What is happening to our humanity? Among other technologies, how are digital media impacting us?

SHAPING FUTURE
GENERATIONS AND OURSELVES

The Fisher-Price iPad Apptivity Seat may be one of the most eloquent, if grotesque, icons of the first quarter of the twenty-first century. "The seat is the ultimate babysitter,"[34] says Campaign for a Commercial-Free Childhood director Susan Linn. The device is a child's car seat with a holder attached for an iPad or other digital device that hovers over the child's face. Advertised for newborns-to-toddlers, some experts argue that the seat is tantamount to giving babies their first hit of digital crack cocaine.

Frighteningly, the past two decades of research on emerging digital media have shown less than positive effects on both adults and children. According to Mari Swingle, instead of perfecting ourselves, "For children, adolescents, and youth, excessive usage of digital media is now highly associated with learning disabilities, emotional dysregulation, as well as conduct and behavior disorders. For adults, it is highly correlated with anxiety, depression, sexual dysfunction and sexual deviation, insomnia, social isolation, disaffected pair bonding, marital conflict, and compromised work performance."[35] Swingle continues:

> The universal place-time accessibility we initially embraced thereafter systematically invaded all aspects of our lives. We are now always "on call": workers, parents, spouses, children, lovers, all of us in (all) our multiple roles. Many of us now do not, or cannot, liberate ourselves from "accessibility" and the buzz of the world. But what is this doing to our brains? The short answer is that our brains are speeding up, but not in a good way. Our neuro-physiological reaction, or functional adaptation, to the age of digital media is a higher state of arousal and the nemesis that comes with [sic]. What nemesis? Quite simply, higher states of arousal come with decreased abilities to self-quiet. Elevated states of arousal are further coupled with a reduced ability to self-stimulate and self-entertain. This includes

reduced abilities to observe, integrate information, and to be creative. In essence, we have less ability to sustain focus on the normal, the baseline, including states of observation, contemplation, and transitions from which ideas spark—what many under the age of twenty now consider a void, proclaiming boredom.

We now feel agitated when not externally stimulated; we need to be occupied, entertained. We also have greater troubles quieting, including reaching states of repose, satisfaction, and restorative sleep.[36]

One expert who has warned about the deleterious effects of digital media on infants and children is Mary Aiken, a cyberpsychologist in Ireland. She and her colleagues at the CyberPsychology Research Network have conducted research and training with INTERPOL, the FBI, and the White House. In a 2015 article in the journal *Psychology Research*, Aiken et al. called for an urgent investigation of the effects of interactive screentime on infants and very young children.[37] In her most recent volume, *The Cyber Effect*, Aiken chronicles ways cyberspace is changing the way we think, feel, and behave.[38] The findings are not comforting.

During the first three months of a baby's postpartum life, her brain will grow a remarkable 20 percent. According to the best brain science, when a baby is born, each cell of the brain has about 2,500 synapses (junctions between two brain cells). In the next three years that number grows to about 15,000 per brain cell. At this stage the brain is creating 700–1,000 new neural connections every second. In other words, the foundation for higher-level brain function is developing robustly during this phase of a baby's life.

We also know that the best way to help a baby develop speech and other cognitive skills is through human interaction. "Time and again videos and television shows have been shown to be ineffective in learning prior to the age of two."[39] Nevertheless, because they tap into our technological optimism, devices like the Apptivity Seat tempt parents to think digital media may be a helpful tool in teaching babies to learn. Just the opposite, they may cause harm. One study of a thousand infants who viewed more than two hours of DVDs per day actually performed worse on language assessments than babies who did not view DVDs.[40]

It is no wonder, then, that in October 2016, the American Academy of Pediatrics offered the following recommendations:

- For children younger than 18 months, avoid use of screen media other than video-chatting. Parents of children 18 to 24 months of age who want to introduce digital media should choose high-quality programming, and watch it with their children to help them understand what they're seeing.

- For children ages 2 to 5 years, limit screen use to 1 hour per day of high-quality programs. Parents should co-view media with children to help them understand what they are seeing and apply it to the world around them.

- For children ages 6 and older, place consistent limits on the time spent using media, and the types of media, and make sure media does not take the place of adequate sleep, physical activity, and other behaviors essential to health.

- Designate media-free times together, such as dinner or driving, as well as media-free locations at home, such as bedrooms.

- Have ongoing communication about online citizenship and safety, including treating others with respect online and offline.[41]

Over against the potential harms of digital exposure, there is strong evidence for the benefits of non-technologically-mediated, unstructured play among children. When a child exercises imagination, creativity, decision-making, and problem-solving, he is helped in developing early math concepts, such as shape, size, and sorting, and, at the same time, fine motor skills and hand-eye coordination.[42]

But the negative impact of digital media is not limited to children. Because of the perception of the lack of authority, the anonymity, and the sense of distance or physical remove, cyberspace facilitates diminished inhibitions among users. What researcher John Suler first called "online disinhibition effect" (ODE) is now an accepted origin of certain behaviors online.[43] ODE contributes not only to impulsive behaviors among some individuals, but also a growing problem with internet addiction. Based on literature review and her own research, Aiken maintains that digital technologies can stimulate the release of dopamine to the pleasure centers of the brain. That explains, in part, why searching online, purchasing goods and services online, and using social media like Instagram, Facebook, and Twitter can be addictive. Aiken writes,

> Hard to resist. That's how many of us find the Internet. It's always delivering a wild surprise, pulsing with breaking news, statistics, personal messages, and entertainment. The overwhelming evidence point to this: A combination of the fast delivery, exploring opportunities, unexpected information, and intermittent rewards creates a medium that is enticing, exciting, and for some individuals totally irresistible. Now let's add in the design aspects of the apps, ads, games, and social-networking sites— the alerts, push notifications, lights, and other visual triggers that signal us like primitive mating calls.[44]

This kind of digitally-induced hyperactivity has also contributed to our inability to find solitude tolerable, much less beneficial. In fact, for increasing numbers of people solitude equals loneliness. Sociologist Sherry Turkle contrasts solitude with loneliness. Solitude is "the capacity to be contentedly and constructively alone," whereas loneliness is a word we invented to describe "the pain of being alone."[45]

> Developmental psychology has long made the case for the importance of solitude. And now so does neuroscience. It is only when we are alone with our thoughts—not reacting to external stimuli—that we engage that part of the brain's basic infrastructure devoted to building up a sense of our stable autobiographical past. This is the "default mode network." So, without solitude, we can't construct a stable sense of self.[46]

But now that connectivity is continuous, fewer and fewer people know how to cope with time alone. They find it difficult to concentrate, they complain of being bored, they get fidgety. In short, they experience anxiety that leads them back to their digital devices, especially their smartphones. Mari Swingle suggests that "A loose yet rather accurate measure of when usage of digital media becomes problematic is (1) when one can't do without, (2) when one can't stop, (3) when one chooses an internet or I-tech activity consistently over all others, and finally, (4) when there is some form of dismissed, or ignored, repercussion or consequence, interpersonally, scholastically, or professionally. In other words, quite simply, when usage starts to have the properties of addiction."[47]

A 2015 study found that Americans check their phones a total of 8 billion times a day, with the average adult checking his or her phone two hundred times a day, or about every five minutes.[48] With more than three quarters of teens having access to smartphones, it's no wonder that digital addiction is rising.[49]

EXCARNATION

Following the lead of Templeton award-winning philosopher Charles Taylor, Australian missiologist Michael Frost has appropriated a vivid term to describe our contemporary technoculture: "excarnation." Frost argues that "the core idea of the Christian faith is the incarnation: God took on flesh and dwelled among us."[50] Jesus of Nazareth is both fully man and fully God. His claim to be God got him crucified on a Roman torture device. His humanity meant that he really died. His divinity meant that he could conquer death and rise from the grave. As the apostle John puts it, "In the beginning was the Word, and the Word was with God, and the Word was God. He was in the beginning with God. ... And the Word became flesh and dwelt among us, and we have seen his glory, glory as of the only Son from the Father, full of grace and truth" (John 1:1–2, 14).

Excarnation is the opposite of incarnation. Historically, excarnation refers to the ancient practice of removing the flesh and organs from a dead body to prepare it for burial. Also known as de-fleshing, the practice was used in the late British Neolithic period in England and Scotland, as well as on the Hawaiian islands as late as the eighteenth century. After rehearsing the history, Frost remarks,

I mention all this not merely to highlight an archaic custom but to suggest that while the defleshing of corpses is no longer in vogue, we currently find ourselves in a time in history where another kind of excarnation occurs, an existential kind in which we are being convinced to embrace an increasingly disembodied presence in our world.[51]

The evidence for excarnation is manifold and damning:

We debate or mock those with whom we disagree on blogs and in social media without ever engaging them face to face. We refer to people who have connected with us on Facebook as our "friends" without necessarily having ever met them. In fact, nothing is more subversively excarnate than the pressure to objectify a stranger as a "friend."

Many teens recognize that they and their friends and family are increasingly tethered to their electronic gadgets, and a substantial number express a desire to disconnect sometimes. A recent study found that 41 percent of teens describe themselves as "addicted" to their phones. Forty-three percent of teens wish that they could "unplug," and more than a third wish they could go back to a time when there was no Facebook.

... [Excarnation] has also seeped into our everyday thinking in the church as well. We drive our SUVs across town to churches in neighborhoods

43

we don't live in (and don't want to). We send SMSs and check Twitter during the sermon, and then we download our favorite celebrity preacher's sermon as a podcast to listen to during the week. ... We sign petitions and change our Facebook profile picture to show our support for various causes without any thought of getting involved personally. We are outraged by those who manipulate child soldiers in Africa or who traffic sex workers from Central Europe, but we don't open our homes to our own neighbors, let alone those with no home at all. And this isn't even to mention the prevalence of online porn usage by churchgoing men, including male clergy.

This says even some church leaders themselves are intentionally excarnate, appearing only onscreen via satellite links, beamed in from the mother church, multiplied and digitized for a consumer audience. It's as though the pastor becomes the new icon in the Protestant worship service.[52]

Although not a professing Christian, cultural critic Lee Siegel offers a similar diagnosis in his broadside, *Against the Machine: Being Human in an Age of the Electronic Mob*:

What kind of idea do we have of the world when, day after day, we sit in front of our screens and enter further and further into the illusion that we ourselves are actually creating our own external reality out of our own internal desires? We become impatient with realities that don't gratify our impulses or satisfy our picture of reality. We find it harder to accept the immutable limitations imposed by identity, talent, personality. We start to behave in public as if we were acting in private, and we begin to fill our private world with gargantuan public appetites. In other words, we find it hard to bear simply being human.

For the first time in human history, a person can have romance, friendship, and sex (sort of); be fed, clothed, and entertained; receive medical, legal, and just about every other type of advice; collect all sorts of information, from historical facts to secrets about other people—all without leaving home. For the first time in human history, a technology exists that allows a person to live as many secret lives, under a pseudonym, as he is able to manage. For the first time in human history, a person can broadcast his opinions, beliefs, and most intimate thoughts—not to mention his face, or any other part of his body—to tens of millions of other people.[53]

4

WAYS FORWARD FOR THOUGHTFUL CHRISTIANS

As I indicated above, despite these profound problems, digital technologies also have profound potential for good. So what is the way forward? Where do we go from here?

First, we should reject uncritical, consumeristic, adoption of digital technologies. We need to establish a set of criteria for employing new digital technologies. In what is a now famous declaration reprinted in *Harpers* magazine, Kentucky agrarian author and farmer Wendell Berry established an argument for why he wasn't going to buy a computer (and, by the way, still hasn't). The short answer is, "I do not see that computers are bringing us one step nearer to anything that does matter to me: peace, economic justice, ecological health, political honesty, family and community stability, good work."[54] In the conclusion of his essay, Berry provided his standards for technological innovation, arguing that any new technological tool should:

- Be cheaper than the one it replaces.

- Be at least as small in scale as the one it replaces.

- Do work that is clearly and demonstrably better than the one it replaces.

- Use less energy than the one it replaces (preferably solar or bodily energy).

- If possible, use some form of solar energy, such as that of the body.

- Be repairable by a person of ordinary intelligence (provided they have the tools).

- Be purchasable/repairable as near to home as possible.

- Come from a small, privately owned shop or store that will take it back for maintenance and repair.

- NOT replace or disrupt anything good that already exists, and this includes family and community relationships.

Although these criteria may seem too restrictive or overly strict, the point is that Berry has a rationale for adopting new technologies. And I would argue that he offers us a good place to begin.

Also, please note that Berry is not a Luddite. The epithet "Luddite" is meant to brand a person as hopelessly antitechnological. But this is not so. Who were the Luddites? They were a group of English craftsmen from Yorkshire who fought back against the industrialization of the woolen industry in the early nineteenth century. They were self-employed and mainly knitted wool hosiery in their homes.

The rise of factories and industrial processes threatened not only their livelihoods, but their entire way of life. Their leader was Ned Ludd, hence, the Luddites. It's not clear whether Ned Ludd was a real or fictitious character, but for those who called themselves Luddites, it didn't matter. What did matter was that they did not reject technology per se. After all, they used hand looms to knit socks for sale. What they rebelled against was mechanization of the process. They had a "form of life" that involved good people, good work, and a familiar way of life. Industrialization would mean large factories, imported employees, and a lifestyle governed more by efficiency than craftsmanship. They were decidedly not opposed to technology, but railed against the disintegration of their communities.

Second, we should remember our humanity. The anthropological benchmarks outlined above should provide some assistance in establishing criteria. That we are the kind of beings who exercise our wills argues that we should be critical and reflective as we think about technology. Moreover, disembodiment or excarnational technologies should be resisted. Likewise, atomistic individualism should be rejected. We belong in community. As Schultze recommends, "We should accept no humanly devised idols as substitutes for God, no Tower of Babel for the heavenly city."[55]

Third, like the modern-day Luddites, the Amish, we should resist the notion that efficiency is the *summum bonum*, the greatest good. In some spheres of life inefficiency should be the measure of the good. For instance, if my wife looked across the table during our candlelit fiftieth anniversary dinner and remarked, "You know, you've been the most efficient husband a woman could wish for," how would I take that? Either it is an insult or a category mistake. Relationships between husbands and wives, parents and children, and pastors and church members are not measured by efficiency but by richness, depth, and time spent cultivating the relationship.

In the same way, discipleship and education are, by their very nature, inefficient enterprises. They are more like the relationship between a parent and a child or between a master craftsman and an apprentice than they are like industrial processes.

5

CONCLUSION

. . . . .

T HESE POINTS BEG for practical ways of moving forward. Thus, in *Reclaiming Conversation*, Turkle suggests that those who wish to tame technology should:

- Remember the power of your phone. It's not an accessory. It's a psychologically potent device that changes not just what you do but who are.

- Slow down.

- Protect your creativity. Take your time and take quiet time. Find your own agenda and keep your own pace.

- Create sacred spaces for conversation.

- Think of unitasking as the next big thing.

- Talk to people with whom you don't agree.

- Obey the seven-minute rule—wait at least seven minutes into a conversation before reaching for your phone.

- Challenge a view of the world as apps.

- Choose the right tool for the job.

- Learn from moments of friction.

- Remember what you know about life.

- Don't avoid difficult conversations.

- Try to avoid all-or-nothing thinking.

Aiken offers the following practical steps:

- Have a device to announce the time (such as a watch), instead of your phone.

- Uninstall beckoning apps.

- Turn off notifications.

- Keep phone in airplane mode.

- Turn your phone off—cold turkey.

- If you must play on an iPad or smartphone, play *with* your child.

Finally, the Sabbath principle may be immensely helpful. Duke University's Norman Wirzba has written in *Living the Sabbath*,

> A Sabbath way of living stands in marked contrast to our current stressful, exhausting, death-wielding ways. According to the psalmist, Sabbath observance is above all infused with thanksgiving and praise. Insofar as our practical living grows out of a grateful disposition, a sense that the gifts of

God to us far exceed what we can comprehend or expect, we give concrete witness to the world of a God whose generosity and care simply know no bounds. When our work and our play, our exertion and our rest flow seamlessly from this deep desire to give thanks to God, the totality of our living—cooking, eating, cleaning, preaching, teaching, parenting, building, repairing, healing creating—becomes one sustained and ever-expanding act of worship.[56]

Whether you call it a digital detox or a digital Sabbath, one way to avoid, or, if necessary, break the addictive power of digital technology is to rest from it. At regular periods, turn it off, walk away, and find rest and delight in God and what God has made, even if it's only for twenty minutes at a time. Ironically, online resources like the Jewish www.sabbathmanifesto.org and the Christian website www.artofmanliness.com offers helpful tips on breaking the cycle of technological addiction. The alternative is to learn the hard way: if we don't get away, we'll come apart.

Acknowledgments

T HE SERIES Questions for Restless Minds is produced by the Christ on Campus Initiative, under the stewardship of the editorial board of D. A. Carson (senior editor), Douglas Sweeney, Graham Cole, Dana Harris, Thomas McCall, Geoffrey Fulkerson, and Scott Manetsch. The editorial board recognizes with gratitude the many outstanding evangelical authors who have contributed to this series, as well as the sponsorship of Trinity Evangelical Divinity School (Deerfield, Illinois), and the financial support of the MAC Foundation and the Carl F. H. Henry Center for Theological Understanding. The editors also wish to thank Christopher Gow, who created the study questions accompanying each book, and Todd Hains, our editor at Lexham Press. May God alone receive the glory for this endeavor!

Study Guide Questions

1. Do you think technology has mostly a positive or negative impact on your life? What about your schedule, specifically? Your mental health? Your attitude toward others?

2. Mitchell presents some shocking statistics about tech use in the United States. When you look at the screen time data on your device, what do you feel?

3. To what extent do you feel that you have a choice as to whether you use digital technologies?

4. How much of your tech use builds your faith? How much of it contributes to your flourishing or the flourishing of others?

5. Review Mitchell's description of what it means to be human on pages 28–32. How does technology enable you to express these human characteristics?

6. How comfortable are you with extended solitude?

7. Review the practical tips on pages 57–59. Would any of these practical steps improve your ability to resist tech addiction or to be more present to the people around you? What are a few steps you could take this week or this month?

For Further Reading

Postman, Neil. *Technopoly: The Surrender of Culture to Technology.* Vintage, 1993.

> A modern classic written by the late media critic and Columbia University professor, *Technopoly* contrasts the Orwellian with the Huxleyan critique of modern culture and argues that media technology (in this case, the television news) dilutes and flattens information making it nearly impossible to sort the acute from the mundane. Much of his analysis can be equally applied to contemporary media.

Swingle, Mari. *i-Minds: How Cell Phones, Computers, Gaming, and Social Media Are Changing Our Brains, Our Behavior, and the Evolution of Our Species.* New Society, 2016.

> An up-to-date review by a Canadian neurotherapist of what we are learning about the way digital technologies form and deform cognitive structures and behavior. Constant connectivity is changing our brains.

Turkle, Sherry. *Alone Together: Why We Expect More from Technology and Less from Each Other*. Basic Books, 2012.

Based on extensive interviews with people from all walks of life, children and adults, MIT social scientist Turkle describes the way technology is impacting human relationships. A deeply unsettling book.

The New Atlantis: A Journal of Technology and Society. http://www.thenewatlantis.com.

Published by the Center for the Study of Technology and Society and The Ethics and Public Policy Center in Washington, DC, the journal seeks to improve public understanding of the social, political, ethical, and policy implications of modern science and technology. A great resource for those seeking to understand the ethical, legal, and social implications of emerging technologies, including digital media.

Schultze, Quentin J. *Habits of the High-tech Heart: Living Virtuously in the Information Age*. Baker Academic, 2004.

Schultze is a renowned media experts who has taught for many years at Calvin College. He argues that we must focus on the cultivation of Christian virtues and practices—the habits of the heart—as we make decisions about social media.

Second Nature. https://secondnaturejournal.com.

> An online journal for critical thinking about technology and new media in light of the Christian tradition, Second Nature is a very thoughtful resource published by The International Institute for the Study of Technology and Christianity lead by directors with a connection to Wheaton College. The journal explores the connection between media and technology, worship, theology, poetry, and contemporary culture.

Bibliography

Aiken, M. *The Cyber Effect: A Pioneering Cyberpsychologist Explains How Human Behavior Changes Online.* Spiegel & Grau, 2016.

Borgmann, A. *Power Failure: Christianity in the Culture of Technology.* Brazos, 2003.

Bourgeois, D. *Ministry in the Digital Age: Strategies and Best Practices for a Post-Website World.* InterVarsity, 2013.

Campbell, H. and Garner, S. *Networked Theology: Negotiating Faith in Digital Culture.* Baker Academic, 2016.

Campbell, H. *Digital Religion: Understanding Religious Practice in New Media Worlds.* Routledge, 2013.

Campbell, H. *When Religion Meets New Media*, Routledge, 2010.

Challies, T. *The Next Story: Life and Faith After the Digital Explosion.* Zondervan, 2011.

Deresiewicz, W. "The End of Solitude." The Chronicle Review, January 20, 2009.

Detweiler, C. *iGods: How Technology Shapes Our Spiritual and Social Lives*. Brazos, 2013.

Dyer, J. *From the Garden to the City: The Redeeming and Corrupting Power of Technology*. Kregel, 2011.

Frost, M. *Incarnate: The Body of Christ in an Age of Disengagement*. InterVarsity, 2014.

Harari, Y. *Homo Deus: A Brief History of Tomorrow*. Harvill Secker, 2016.

Hipps, S. *Flickering Pixels: How Technology Shapes Your Faith*. Zondervan, 2009.

Houston, G. *Virtual Morality: Christian Ethics in the Computer Age*. Apollos, 1998.

Hunt, A. *Surviving Technopolis: Essays on Finding Balance in Our New Man-Made Environments*. Pickwick, 2013.

Jasanoff, S. *The Ethics of Invention: Technology and the Human Future*. Norton, 2016.

Kallenberg, B. *God and Gadgets: Following Jesus in a Technological Age*. Cascade, 2011.

Kelly, K. *The Inevitable: Understanding the 12 Technological Forces that Will Shape Our Future*. Viking, 2016.

Latham, B. *iPod, YouTube, Wii Play: Theological Engagements with Entertainment*. Cascade, 2012.

Leonhard, G. *Technology vs. Humanity: The Coming Clash Between Man and Machine*. Fast Future, 2016.

Lynch, J. *The Scent of Lemons: Technology and Relationships in the Age of Facebook*. Darton, Longman & Todd, 2012.

Lynch, M. *The Internet of Us: Knowing More and Understanding Less in the Age of Big Data.* Doubleday, 2016.

Monsma, S. *Responsible Technology: A Christian Perspective.* Eerdmans, 1986.

Perlow, L. *Sleeping with Your Smartphone: How to Break the 24/7 Habit and Change the Way You Work.* Harvard Business Review Press, 2012.

Powers, W. *Hamlet's Blackberry: A Practical Philosophy for Building a Good Life in the Digital Age.* Harper, 2010.

Schultze, Q. *Habits of the High-Tech Heart: Living Virtuously in the Information Age.* Baker Academic, 2002.

Schuurman, D. *Shaping a Digital World: Faith, Culture and Computer Technology.* IVP Academic, 2013.

Siegel, L. *Against the Machine: Being Human in the Age of the Electronic Mob.* Spiegel & Grau, 2008.

Smith, C. *What is a Person? Rethinking Humanity, Social Life, and the Moral Good From the Person Up.* University of Chicago Press, 2010.

Spadaro, A. *Cybertheology: Thinking Christianity in the Era of the Internet.* Fordham, 2014.

Swingle, M. *i-Minds: How Cell Phones, Computers, Gaming, and Social Media Are Changing Our Brains, Our Behavior, and the Evolution of Our Species.* New Society, 2016.

Turkle, S. *Reclaiming Conversation: The Power of Talk in a Digital Age*. Penguin, 2015.

Vallor, S. *Technology and the Virtues: A Philosophical Guide to a Future Worth Wanting*. Oxford University Press, 2016.

Waters, B. *Christian Moral Theology in the Emerging Technoculture: From Posthuman Back to Human*. Ashgate, 2014.

Notes

1. Stephen Monsma, ed., *Responsible Technology: A Christian Perspective* (Eerdmans, 1986).
2. Jacques Ellul, *The Technological Society* (Knopf, 1964).
3. Kevin Kelly, *The Inevitable: Understanding the 12 Technological Forces that Will Shape Our Future* (Viking, 2016), 4.
4. *Digital Media and Society: Implications in a Hyper-connected Era* (World Economic Forum, 2015), 5. http://www3.weforum.org/docs/WEFUSA_ DigitalMediaAndSociety_Report2016.pdf.
5. Christian Smith, *What is a Person? Rethinking Humanity, Social Life, and the Moral Good From the Person Up* (University of Chicago Press, 2010).
6. Mari Swingle, *i-Minds: How Cell Phones, Computers, Gaming, and Social Media Are Changing Our Brains, Our Behavior, and the Evolution of Our Species* (New Society, 2016), 5.
7. Heidi A. Campbell, ed., *Digital Religion: Understanding Religious Practice in New Media Worlds* (Routledge, 2013).

8. David T. Bourgeois, *Ministry in the Digital Age: Strategies and Best Practices for a Post-Website World* (IVP, 2013), 8.

9. Bourgeois, *Ministry in the Digital Age*, 9.

10. Bourgeois, *Ministry in the Digital Age*, 11.

11. "Churches Divided on Website Usage," Lifeway Research, January 2010, http://lifewayresearch. com/wp-content/uploads/2011/01/DOC_ ChurchesDividedonWebsiteUsage.pdf

12. "Cyber Church: Pastors and the Internet," Barna Group, February 11, 2015, https://www.barna.com/ research/cyber-church-pastors-and-the-internet/.

13. "Plan grows to put WiFi in every church," *Church Times*, January 9, 2015, https://www.churchtimes .co.uk/articles/2015/9-january/news/uk/plans- grow-to-put-wifi-in-every-church.

14. Heidi A. Campbell and Stephen Garner, *Networked Theology: Negotiating Faith in Digital Culture* (Baker Academic, 2016), 117.

15. Michael Patrick Lynch, *The Internet of Us: Knowing More and Understanding Less in the Age of Big Data* (Doubleday), 2016.

16. Lynch, *The Internet of Us*, 23.

17. Kristin Purcell and Lee Rainie, *Technology's Impact on Workers*, Pew Research Center, December 30, 2014, http://www.pewinternet.org/2014/12/30 /technologys-impact-on-workers/.

18. Jennifer Buchanan, Beth Kelley, and Alicia Hatch, "Digital workplace and culture: digital technologies are changing the workforce and how enterprises can adapt and evolve," Deloitte Digital, 2016, 2. https://www2.deloitte.com/content/dam/Deloitte/us/Documents/human-capital/us-cons-digital-workplace-and-culture.pdf.

19. Shane Hipps, *Flickering Pixels: How Technology Shapes Your Faith* (Zondervan, 2009), 13.

20. Hipps, *Flickering Pixels*, 167.

21. Hipps, *Flickering Pixels*, 169. Italics original.

22. Campbell, *Digital Religion*, 1.

23. Josh Bersin, "Use of MOOCs And Online Education Is Exploding: Here's Why," *Forbes*, January 5, 2016, http://www.forbes.com/sites/joshbersin/2016/01/05/use-of-moocs-and-online-education-is-exploding-heres-why/#73bd8d9e7f09.

24. http://www.chronicle.com/article/How-Elite-Universities/229233/.

25. Transhumanists maintain that the current phase of humanity is transitional, hence trans-human. The trajectory of human technological self-evolution is towards being post-human. See C. Ben Mitchell, Edmund Pellegrino, Jean Bethke Elshtain, et al., *Biotechnology and the Human Good* (Georgetown University Press, 2007) and Brent Waters, "Whose Salvation? Which Eschatology? Transhumanism

and Christianity as Contending Salvific Religions" in *Transhumanism and Transcendence: Christian Hope in an Age of Technological Enhancement*, ed. Ronald Cole-Turner (Georgetown University Press, 2011).

26. Katherine Hayles, *How We Became Posthuman: Virtual Bodies in Cybernetics, Literature, and Informatics* (University of Chicago Press, 1999), 283.

27. Michael Novak, *The Fire of Invention: Civil Society and the Future of the Corporation* (Rowman & Littlefield, 1999).

28. David E. Nye, "Shaping Communication Networks: Telegraph, Telephone, Computer," in *Technology and the Rest of Culture*, ed. Arien Mack (Ohio State University Press, 1997), 125.

29. James K. A. Smith, *You Are What You Love: The Spiritual Power of Habit* (Brazos, 2016).

30. Yuval Noah Harari, *Homo Deus: A Brief History of Tomorrow* (Harvill Secker, 2016), 273.

31. Harari, *Homo Deus*, 368.

32. Harari, *Homo Deus*.

33. Harari, *Homo Deus*, 49.

34. "Baby Bouncy Seat with iPad Attachment Sparks Outrage Online," *CBS News*, December 10, 2013. http://www.cbsnews.com/news/baby-bouncy -seat-with-ipad-attachment-sparks-outrage-online/.

35. Swingle, *i-Minds*, xii.

36. Swingle, *i-Minds*, xviii-xix.

37. Ciaran Haughton, Mary Aiken, and Carly Cheevers, "Cyber Babies: The Impact of Emerging Technology on the Developing Infant," *Psychology Research* 5 (September 2015), 504–18.

38. Mary Aiken, *The Cyber Effect: A Pioneering Cyberpsychologist Explains How Human Behavior Changes Online* (Spiegel & Grau), 2016.

39. Aiken, *The Cyber Effect*, 97.

40. Aiken, *The Cyber Effect*, 98.

41. "Media and Young Minds," Council on Communications and Media, Pediatrics, 138.5 (2016), http://pediatrics.aappublications.org/content/138/5/e20162591.

42. Aiken, *The Cyber Effect*, 102.

43. Aiken, *The Cyber Effect*, 22.

44. Aiken, *The Cyber Effect*, 53.

45. Sherry Turkle, *Reclaiming Conversation: The Power of Talk in a Digital Age* (Penguin, 2015), 65.

46. Turkle, *Reclaiming Conversation*, 61.

47. Swingle, *i-Minds*, 10.

48. Aiken, *The Cyber Effect*, 54.

49. *Teens, Social Media & Technology Overview 2015*, Pew Research Center, April 9, 2015, http://www.pewinternet.org/2015/04/09/teens-social-media-technology-2015/.

50. Michael Frost, *Incarnate: The Body of Christ in an Age of Disengagement* (IVP, 2014), 15.

51. Frost, *Incarnate*, 10.

52. Frost, *Incarnate*, 24–25.

53. Lee Siegel, *Against the Machine: Being Human in an Age of the Electronic Mob* (Spiegel & Grau, 2008), 18, 21.

54. For the complete essay, see Wendell Berry, *What Are People For?* (North Point, 1990), 170–77.

55. Quentin J. Schultze, *Habits of the High-tech Heart: Living Virtuously in the Information Age* (Baker Academic, 2004), 197.

56. Norman Wirzba, *Living the Sabbath: Discovering the Rhythms of Rest and Delight* (Brazos, 2006), 21.

QUESTIONS FOR RESTLESS MINDS